How To Handle Grown-ups

STOP CHILDREN

D1350732

Scholastic Children's Books,
Commonwealth House, 1–19 New Oxford Street,
London WC1A 1NU, UK
a division of Scholastic Ltd
London ~ New York ~ Toronto ~ Sydney ~ Auckland
Mexico City ~ New Delhi ~ Hong Kong

This edition produced for the Book People Ltd,
Hall Wood Avenue, Haydock, St Helens WA11 9UL

First published in the UK by Scholastic Ltd, 2003

How To Handle Grown-ups

By Roy Apps

Illustrated by Jo Moore

Contents

It was a dark and stormy night...
and the rain was coming down in buckets –
tin ones rather than plastic ones at that – and
the wind was whistling in the trees. I went
over to the window and gasped with horror,
who happened to be with me at the time.

ME   HORROR

There, leering at me, was a truly hideous
face with great big ears and beady eyes. I
stuck my tongue out at it – and it stuck out its
tongue back. I looked at it fiercely. It looked
fiercely back at me. All of a sudden, I realized
I was looking at my own reflection. And not
only that, my own reflection was looking
back at me.

I went across to shut the curtains on the
other window and gasped with horror again.
There was another face – and if this one was

7

my reflection I was in big trouble, because it was a *girl's* face!

Then the girl began to speak, but I couldn't hear what she was saying.

"I can't hear you!" I yelled. But she couldn't hear me either.

So the girl blew on to the window and wrote a message in her breath. It said:

Can I come in?

I opened the window and let her in.

"Sorry to just drip in like this," she said.

"Not to worry," I replied. "What are you doing out on a night like this?"

"I think I'm lost," the girl said, "I was trying to find number 13 Tenby Gardens."

I knew Tenby Gardens well. They were next to Elevenby Gardens.

"If you go up to the high street, turn first left by the second-hand shop, then third right by the first-hand shop you're halfway there."

"Thanks," said the girl. She started to climb back out through the window. "I'm going to get soaked through!" she muttered.

"Are you?" I enquired. "When?"

"Now!" answered the girl. "It's pouring hard out there. If you don't believe me, just put your head out of the window and see for yourself."

I tried doing what the girl suggested, but it was no use. "Sorry," I said, "I can't put my head out. It seems to be attached to my shoulders. Tell you what, why don't you stay here until the rain eases off? I'll hang your coat up."

Once the girl had managed to wriggle off the coat peg, we went through to the sitting room.

"I haven't told you my name, have I?" said the girl.

"I don't think you have," I said. "Just let me check through the last couple of pages... No, you're right. You haven't."

"I'm Anna," said the girl.

"Would that be Anna Conda?"

Anna nodded.

"I thought it might be," I said.

"The thing is," Anna went on, "me and my mates want some advice on how to handle Groan-ups."

"Don't you mean Grown-ups?"

"I know what I mean," said Anna. "As soon as a Grown-up enters a room I want to groan."

"Hmmm, you feel put upon and hard done by?" I enquired.

"Too right we do," said Anna. "They're always telling us what to do, and going on about how things were different when they were our age. And they're so bossy and uncool. Apparently, there's this guy who lives at number 13 Tenby Gardens who can help you handle Grown-ups. Apparently he's dead mysterious and no one knows his real name."

I nodded. "I think I know who you mean," I replied. "Have you ever heard of the Scarlet Pimpernel?"

"He was a hero who helped a lot of people during the French Revolution, wasn't he?" replied Anna.

"That's right," I said. "Those people felt put upon and hard done by too. Mainly because they kept getting thrown into dungeons and losing things. Like their heads."

"So what's the Scarlet Pimpernel got to do with this mysterious guy who can help me and my mates handle Grown-ups?" asked Anna, not unreasonably.

"The person you are looking for," I replied, "is a distant descendant of the Scarlet Pimpernel."

Anna gasped. "You mean he's a kind of modern fearless and daring hero?"

I nodded.

"And is he called the Scarlet Pimpernel after his famous ancestor?" asked Anna.

"No," I replied. "He's called the Scarlet Pimplenose. After his nose."

Anna frowned and stared at me. In particular, she stared at the scarlet pimple on the end of my nose.

"You?" she exclaimed. She frowned. "You don't look daring and fearless."

"Oh?"

"Gormless, maybe, but definitely not fearless."

"That's all part of my disguise," I explained. "Now do you and your mates want help with handling Grown-ups or not?"

"Yes, please," said Anna, desperately.

"Meet me at nine o'clock tomorrow morning," I instructed.

"Where?" asked Anna.

"Well, I must be careful that no stray Grown-ups see me," I said.

"Why, what would they do to you?" asked Anna. "Throw you in a dungeon?"

"No, they'd laugh at the pimple on my nose," I replied.

"Well, where's the place you would least expect to find yourself?" suggested Anna.

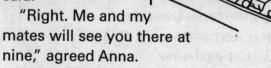
Me

I thought for a moment. "The top floor of the multi-storey car park," I said.

"Right. Me and my mates will see you there at nine," agreed Anna.

"Good. I'll have a luxury coach ready and waiting," I added.

"A luxury coach?" Anna frowned.

"If you and your mates are to become genuine Grown-up handlers, first of all you'll need to study them in captivity," I explained. "And that will require us to go on a coach trip."

And so, the very next day...
I stood on the top floor of the multi-storey car park and suddenly remembered why it

12

was the last place I'd think of finding myself –
I was scared of heights!

My knees started
shaking like a
jelly. My whole
body started
quivering like a
blancmange. I was
turning into a trifle!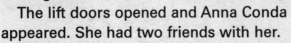

The lift doors opened and Anna Conda
appeared. She had two friends with her.

"These are my mates. This is Barry Cuda,"
she said, indicating a boy with a toothy
smile. "And this," she said, pointing to the
other boy, "is Tony Arm-Legg."

"Pleased to meet you," I said. "Come on!
All aboard! It's time we were going."

Anna frowned. "You said we were going
on a luxury coach."

"That's right," I said.

"That's not a luxury coach," she said.
"That's a luxury couch!"

"I know," I said. "I did the booking on the
Internet and typed in couch instead of coach."
I shrugged. "Shall we get this thing on the
road?"

Anna and her mates jumped on to the
couch. I gave it an almighty shove and
jumped on too.

We sped out of the multi-storey car park and on through the town. Ten minutes later we were approaching our destination.

"Hit the brakes!" I yelled.

Then I remembered something: the luxury couch didn't have any brakes. So we hit the gates instead. And the gates hit us back.

"Have we arrived?" asked Barry.

"Of course we have," I replied. "Can't you see what the sign says?"

"Yes, it says '*!*!*!$?!**'," said Barry, whose head had taken the full force of our collision with the gates.

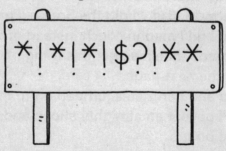

What the sign actually said was:

Welcome to the Grown-up Safari Park

ALL KINDS OF GROWN-UPS ON DISPLAY

○ LAUGH AT THE ANTICS OF THE WALLY-BIES

○ GASP AT THE BEHAVIOUR OF THE
   KANGA-RUDES!!

ALL VISITORS ENTER THIS PARK
ENTIRELY AT THEIR OWN RISK!

"Now follow me," I said, "and I'll take you to where our first lesson in Grown-up handling will begin."

"Where's that?" asked Anna.

"On the next page..." I said.

How To Handle Grown-ups: Stage One

Learning About the Different Types of Grown-ups

"There are three main types of Grown-ups on display in the park," I explained. I pointed to a large board at the side of the path. It yawned at me...

(So, it really was bored.)

"There is your Wild Grown-up..."

"So called because—"

"They're wild?" suggested Tony.

I shook my head. "So called because the things they do make *us* wild. They live in the least scary bits of the Safari Park, known as Level One. Then further on in the park, in the area known as Level Two, where the trees are denser and it's dark and dingy, roam the Even Wilder Grown-ups."

"The things they get up to make us even wilder. And then in the darkest, most remote part of the park known as Level Three you will find..."

Anna and Barry shivered.

"...the Wildest Grown-ups!"

"Can we start with the Wildest Grown-ups?" asked Tony. "They sound really gruesome."

I shook my head. "The Wildest Grown-ups are the most difficult to handle," I said. "You must learn how to handle Wild Grown-ups and Even Wilder Grown-ups first."

"Then what are we waiting for?" asked Tony, pouting.

"Oh dear, you sound a little testy," I told him. "But that's quite appropriate really, because a little testy is what I've got for you. A little testy on what you've learnt so far."

The Scarlet Pimplenose's Little Testy on Different Types of Grown-ups.

The following captions and pictures have been mixed up. Can you match the right ones?

1. A WILD GROWN-UP

(a)

2. AN EVEN WILDER GROWN-UP

(b)

3. A WILDEST GROWN-UP

(c)

4. A WEIRD GROWN-UP

(d)

5. A WEED GROWN-UP

(e)

ANSWERS: 1. (c); 2. (d); 3. (e); 4. (b); 5. (a)

SCORING: Take five points for every right answer and minus five points for every left answer.

HOW DID YOU RATE ON THE SCARLET PIMPLENOSE'S LITTLE TESTY?
25 points: Well done, top of the class! You are now ready to proceed with the next stage of the Scarlet Pimplenose's Grown-up Handling Course!

15–20 points: Top of the class – Reception Class that is.

5 pints: Are you sure that's your little testy result and not your mum's note to the milkman?

How To Handle Grown-ups: Stage Two

The Wild Grown-up

Wild Grown-up Species No. 1: The Water Duffer-lo

I led Anna, Barry and Tony down the path a short distance to a large pond.

"Here we are in Level One," I explained. "The water creatures are down here. They're the really wet Grown-ups. Ah! Just as I thought! There's a typical Wild Grown-up."

"What, do you mean the old man who's fishing?" asked Tony.

I nodded. "His name's Mr Wally Questions and he's a species of Grown-up known as the Water Duffer-lo," I said. "Not to be confused with a water buffalo."

WATER BUFFALO   WATER DUFFER-LO

"Oh no! He's seen us! How did that happen?" asked Anna.

"It might have something to do with the fact that Barry's been shouting 'Ner, ner, who's a Water Duffer-lo?' at him for the last ten seconds," I suggested. "But don't worry. He's completely harmless."

Mr Wally Questions came up to me. "Hello, Scarlet Pimplenose," he said. "My, you have grown since I last saw you!"

Anna, Barry and Tony started sniggering and I was considering which one of them to chuck in the pond first when another Wild Grown-up appeared and started running towards us.

"It's Mrs Utterly-Crazy," I said. "She's another Duffer-lo. And she's crackers."

QUACKERS

CRACKERS

Mrs Utterly-Crazy went straight up to Anna, Barry and Tony. "Hello," she trilled. "Looking forward to going back to school after the holidays?"

We made our way to a small clearing in the woods.

"They won't follow us here, will they?" asked Tony.

I shook my head.

"Good!" said Anna. "I mean, 'Looking forward to going to back to school after the holidays?' That's just what our next-door neighbour, Miss McGoon, is always saying to me! Can you imagine a more idiotic thing to say?"

"Only 'My, you have grown since I last saw you'," I suggested.

"My gran's friend, Mr O'Twitty, is always saying that to me!" said Barry. "It's stupid!

Does he think I'm going to start shrinking, or something?"

"Then it's obvious that Miss McGoon and Mr O'Twitty are both Duffer-loes," I said.

"OK," said Anna, "so how do we handle them?"

"Good question," I answered. "Unlike the questions asked by Duffer-loes."

Water Duffer-lo Handling Technique: The Scarecrow Solution

You are most likely to come across Duffer-lo Grown-ups at home. Typically they're neighbours or friends of your parents or grandparents. They don't really take much notice of you as a person. If they did, they would see you squirm like a worm each time they say "My, you have grown" or "Looking forward to going back to school after the holidays?"

So all you have to do is to put up a picture of yourself on a stick. Then if your Duffer-lo Grown-up is a neighbour, put it by the fence. Or if your Duffer-lo Grown-up is a friend of your gran's, say, put it up by the front door.

Then next time the Duffer-lo appears, he or she can say "My, you have grown" or "Looking forward to going back to school after the holidays?" to the picture on a stick till their heart's content. (Usually about five hours.)

A handy cut-out face can be found on the reverse of this page.

"Brilliant!" said Anna.

"Yes, I am rather, aren't I?" I said, modestly.

Your very own personal scarecrow solution "mask" to cut out and stick on a stick. Why not colour in the eyes and add freckles, broken teeth or runny egg marks on the chin to make it more life-like.

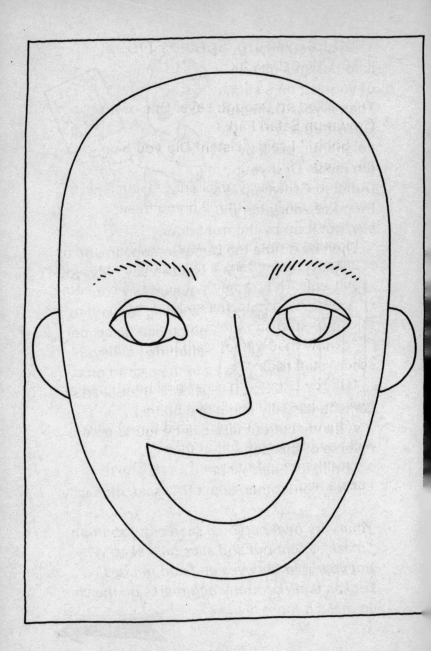

Wild Grown-up Species No. 2: The Yak-erty-yak

We walked on through Level One of the Grown-up Safari Park.

"Shhh!" I said. "Listen! Did you hear anything?"

"Yes!" said Barry, excitedly. "I can hear someone saying 'Shhh did you hear anything!'"

I looked away to give Anna and Tony the chance to shove Barry's head down a nearby rabbit hole. They'd only got as far as his ears when the noise became so loud they were forced to stop and look up.

"I know that sound," said Tony. "It's a school staff room!"

"It's my Grown-up sister and her mates on their mobile phones!" said Anna.

"Ghyuk mubber glug!" said Barry, who still had his mouth full of grass.

"It's the sound of Yak-erty-yak Grown-ups," I explained.

YAK   YAK-ERTY-YAK

27

"Yak-erty-yak Grown-ups never stop talking," I said.

Eventually, the group of Yak-erty-yak Grown-ups passed us by.

"There, they're going now," said Anna, sighing with relief.

"Yes, and they're still going on and on and on!" complained Barry.

"Teach us how to handle Yak-erty-yak Grown-ups, Pimplenose," pleaded Tony. "In as few words as possible," he added.

Yak-erty-yak Handling Technique: The Echo-chamber Solution

The only way to get Yak-erty-yak Grown-ups to stop yakking is to get them to listen to how they sound – ie build an echo chamber. To do this you need a large bowl or bucket, a long stick, a tube of superglue and a Scout or Guide.

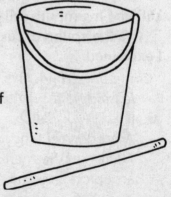

1. Take a large bowl or bucket.
2. Stick it to the end of a long stick (the stick you used for handling Duffer-lo Grown-ups will do very nicely).

3. Lift up the stick and hold the bowl over the Yak-erty-yak's head.
4. The sound of their yakking will echo round in their ears and they will realize just how dreadful they sound!

The DISADVANTAGE of The Echo-chamber Solution

Unfortunately, with an echo chamber over their heads the Yak-erty-yaks can't see where they are going and will crash into nearby trees, lampposts and probably each other, too. First aid may be needed, which is where the Scout or Guide will come in handy.

Wild Grown-up Species No. 3: The Moan-key

"Come on," I said. "It's time we had a break."
   We made our way to the Level One picnic area.
   "What do you fancy to eat?" I asked.
   "What's on the menu?" asked Anna.
   Barry picked up the menu. "Two squashed

flies and a splodge of half-chewed cheese," he replied.

"Don't fancy any of that," said Tony. So we all shared a packet of sour-cream-and-onion flavoured crisps I had brought with me instead.

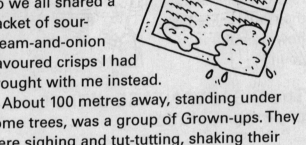

About 100 metres away, standing under some trees, was a group of Grown-ups. They were sighing and tut-tutting, shaking their heads in despair and generally moaning.

"What kind of Grown-ups are those?" asked Anna.

"They're Moan-keys," I replied. "They're a very annoying species of Wild Grown-up who do nothing but moan about your habits all the time. And the really annoying thing is that their habits are even worse than yours!"

MONKEYS   MOAN-KEYS

Some Typical Moan-Key Gripes:

THE MOAN

"The state of your bedroom – it's a tip!"

THE REALITY

Have you seen the state of your dad's shed?

"Shouldn't you be reading *113 Ways to Easy Exam Revision* instead of Hot Hits?"

And what is your mum reading? *Hello!* magazine, of course!

"If you spend any longer watching TV you'll get square eyes."

Do you know how many hours your mum and dad spend watching TV when you're asleep in bed?

"You're not going out in *that?*"

Have you seen the jacket your dad goes down to the pub in?

"Don't put your elbows on the table, it's rude."

"OK, Scarlet Pimplenose," sighed Tony. "What's the solution?"

Moan-key Handling Technique: The Moan-in Solution

"That's the solution," I said, pointing to the group of Moan-keys under the trees. "If there's one thing Moan-keys like better than moaning to you, it's moaning to other Moan-keys *about* you! What you and your friends need to do is to get all the Moan-keys you know together and let them have a good moan amongst themselves. That way you will be left in peace. You can use this all-purpose invitation. Genuine Moan-key Grown-ups won't be able to resist it!"

> ### KIDS DRIVING YOU MAD?
>
> • Then join like-minded Grown-ups for a Mammoth Moaning Moan In!
>
> • Bring your own bottle (Gripe Water provided)
>
> • Contact Mrs Whinge (fill in your address or your friend's address here)
>
> • Date : . . . .

"Right!" I said. "Now we've finished the crisps, we should be in good shape for the next part of our trip through the Grown-up Safari Park. It's time to move on to Level Two and meet some Even Wilder Grown-ups!"

How To Handle Grown-Ups: Stage Three

The Even Wilder Grown-up

We walked on into a darker and denser part of the park, then turned a corner, and...

"Oh my goodness, I see what you mean!" exclaimed Anna.

"I also say what I mean," I added. For there, a little way off in front of us, were two Grown-ups; a man wearing combat trousers, Reebok trainers and a back-to-front baseball cap and a woman in a cut-off top, flares and wrap-around shades.

"Pretty gross, eh?" I suggested.

"Not so sure about the pretty," said Anna. "What species of Even Wilder Grown-up are they?"

"They are Wally-bies," I replied.

Even Wilder Grown-up Species No. 1: The Wally-by

WALLABY

WALLY-BY

"Wally-bies are a really embarrassing species of Grown-up, who try to pretend they're young," I explained.

"That sounds just like my Uncle Sebastian," declared Barry. "Let me tell you what happened last weekend when I went to his place."

So, because we were all feeling in a kindly mood and Barry obviously needed to get something very painful off his chest – and I don't mean Tony who was sitting on it at the time – we agreed to let him tell us his gruesome story.

Barry's Story

I was looking forward to seeing my Uncle Sebastian. I rather hoped we'd have a chocolate-fudge ice cream speed-eating competition like we'd had the last time I'd gone to his place. Or that he'd get his

collection of old Thunderbirds *comics down
from the attic. Instead, he raced out shouting,*

"Hi, Baz, you cool dud!"

"What?" I said, though I guess he meant
dude.

"Wanna play some
garage music?"

Then he tried to
high-five me. Only
he missed, spun
round, and fell over
on his bottom.

Then instead of
swearing, or looking
embarrassed, he said
"Cool!" again.

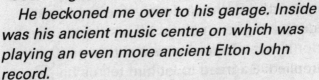

He beckoned me over to his garage. Inside
was his ancient music centre on which was
playing an even more ancient Elton John
record.

"Garage music! Funky or what?" he said.

I mean, talk about embarrassing.

"Oh, Barry, you poor thing," Anna said.

I felt sorry for Barry, too. "Here," I said.
"I've got just the thing for you." From my bag
I took out a chocolate-fudge ice cream.

"Thank you so much, Scarlet Pimplenose,"
said Barry. And he didn't even seem to mind

the fact that because the ice cream had been in my bag all morning it was completely melted.

"The thing is," said Tony. "We need to learn how to handle these Wally-by Grown-ups."

"Right away," I said. "Now what you need to do is—"

Suddenly, the sound of laughter reached our ears

"Quick, hide!" I said.

"Where?" asked Barry.

"Behind this tree!"

We all raced over to a nearby tree.

"It's not big enough for us all to hide behind," said Anna, despairingly.

"It is if we hide this way," I replied. So Barry stood on Anna's shoulders, Tony stood on Barry's shoulders and I stood on Tony's shoulders.

"Who *are* those Grown-ups?" asked Tony.

"And why are they laughing?" asked Barry.

"Aaargh ... ow ... aw..." said Anna, who was slowly sinking into the ground with the weight of us all on her shoulders.

"They're a kind of Grown-up who are similar to Wally-bies, but different in one crucial respect," I explained. "Whereas Wally-bies try and pretend to like fashion and all the latest bands, these Grown-ups laugh at your taste in music and clothes and are really rude about it. That's why they're known as Kanga-rudes.

Even Wilder Grown-up Species No. 2: The Kanga-rude

KANGAROO   KANGA-RUDE

"If they caught sight of us now, they'd fall about laughing," I added.

So we kept quiet until the Kanga-rudes had gone. Luckily Anna had stopped moaning about the weight of us all on her shoulders. Mainly because she was up to her nose in the ground.

Barry said, "OK, Anna, I'll pull you out of the ground now!"

This was unfortunate, for two reasons.
1. Barry had forgotten that Tony and I were standing on his shoulders, so as soon as he *bent* down, we, so to speak, *went* down.
2. The sound of us going ...

Aaq...

qaa...

rgh!

... had alerted the Kanga-rudes to our predicament and there they were, laughing their heads off.

"Ha ha! Kids!" said one.

"Ho ho! Daft as brushes the lot of them," said another.

When they had gone, Barry said, "What did he mean, 'daft as brushes'?"

"It's just a saying," I said.

"Maybe," reasoned Barry. "But have you ever actually *seen* a daft brush?"

I had to admit I hadn't.

"There you are then," said Barry. "To my mind, brushes aren't daft at all. They are very sensible things. Very useful for sweeping up and stuff."

"Can we get back to the issue in question," interrupted Tony. "Which is, how do we handle Kanga-rudes?"

"And don't forget the Wally-bies," added Anna.

"If only we could," sighed Barry.

"I've asked the world's number-one expert on handling Wally-bies and Kanga-rudes to join us," I explained. "She was one of my very first Grown-up-handling students. Ah, here she comes now!"

Through the undergrowth crashed a lithe figure in tracksuit, trainers and fluorescent headband.

Unfortunately, her headband had slipped down over her eyes, which was why she *crashed* through the undergrowth.

"Allow me to introduce May Kaloadadosh!" I announced.

Wally-by and Kanga-rude Handling Technique: The Earn Extra Pocket Money Solution

"Hi!" said May. "Now I want you to put all thoughts of Wally-bies and Kanga-rudes to one side for the moment."

"Would that be to the left side or the right side?" asked Barry.

May shot him a withering look, but he ducked just in time.

"Instead, think about wallabies and kangaroos," said May.

So we all thought about them.

"Funny old creatures, aren't they," May went on, "hopping about like that, *boing, boing.* But Wally-bies and Kanga-rudes are actually even funnier old creatures!"

"Now people will pay good money to go to a zoo or a safari park and see wallabies and kangaroos. So why shouldn't people pay good money to go and see families of Wally-bies and Kanga-rudes? Next time your parents have a barbecue, invite all your friends to come and see these funny old creatures. Let me show you what I mean."

May took a photo from her pocket to show us.

"This is a photo I took at my mum and dad's barbecue," said May.

Everyone started laughing. Well, it was difficult to know which Grown-ups in the photo looked the silliest. The Wally-bies with their trendy clothes or the Kanga-rudes with their naff clothes.

"Who are the people peering over the fence?" asked Anna.

"Three of my friends," said May. "I charged them 50p each to come and have a good laugh. I made £10.50 that night."

"Hang on, three 50p's is only £1.50," frowned Tony.

"I know. I also charged three of my enemies £3 each to come and have a good laugh, too."

Anna didn't look convinced. "But you could only do this once or twice. I mean people won't pay to see the same thing over and over again."

"Ah," smiled May. "That's where...

Another Wally-by Handling Technique: The Earn Even More Extra Pocket Money Solution

...comes in."

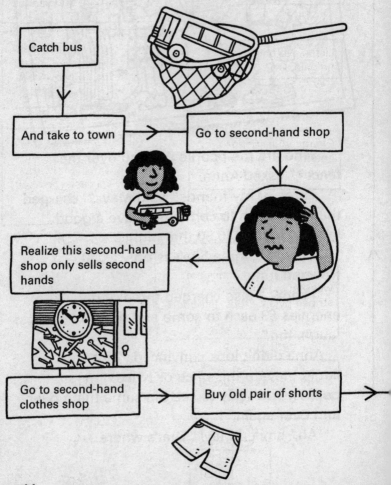

Catch bus

And take to town → Go to second-hand shop

Realize this second-hand shop only sells second hands ←

Go to second-hand clothes shop → Buy old pair of shorts →

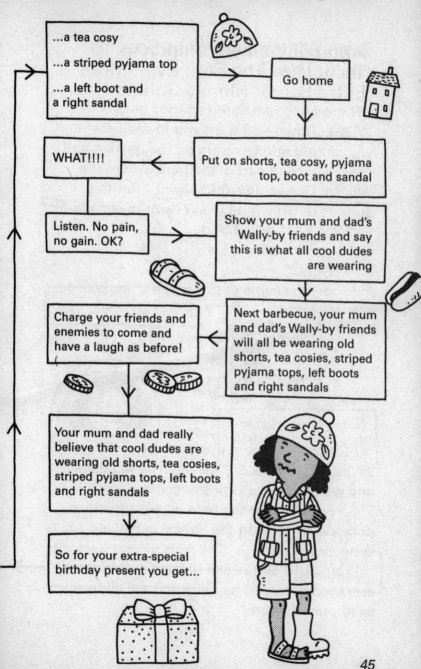

...a tea cosy

...a striped pyjama top

...a left boot and a right sandal

→ Go home

Put on shorts, tea cosy, pyjama top, boot and sandal

WHAT!!!!

Listen. No pain, no gain. OK?

Show your mum and dad's Wally-by friends and say this is what all cool dudes are wearing

Charge your friends and enemies to come and have a laugh as before!

Next barbecue, your mum and dad's Wally-by friends will all be wearing old shorts, tea cosies, striped pyjama tops, left boots and right sandals

Your mum and dad really believe that cool dudes are wearing old shorts, tea cosies, striped pyjama tops, left boots and right sandals

So for your extra-special birthday present you get...

Even Wilder Grown-up Species No. 3: The G-no

"There's one remaining species of Even Wilder Grown-up I want you to see before we venture into Level Three, the darkest and most terrifying part of the park, where the Wildest Grown-ups lurk," I said. "But this species of Grown-up won't want to see you."

"Won't it?" asked Barry.

"G-no," I replied.

"Pardon?"

"That's the name of this species," I explained. "The G-no."

GNU

G-NO

"G-nos are Grown-ups who are always saying 'no'. Come on, we can hide in this hide and wait for some G-nos to come along."

So we all hid in the hide where a warning poster alerted us to the typical behaviour of G-no Grown-ups.

Warning!!! G-nos can behave in totally outrageous ways. The following are all true examples. Beware!

UTTERLY REASONABLE QUESTION

G-NO'S UTTERLY UNREASONABLE ANSWER

To a dad:

To a teacher:

To a next-door neighbour:

To a Grown-up sister:

Can I use your eyeliner to draw my Frankenstein mask?

G-no

Anna, Barry and Tony read the list and sighed. "G-no Grown-ups really are a g-knotty problem," Anna said.

Just then we heard voices outside the hide. We looked through the window. There was a determined-looking lad and a couple of Grown-ups.

"That's Mo Khan," I said. "He recently did the Grown-up Handling Course. Looks like he's a got a couple of G-nos with him who he's going to try and handle."

"Can he do that?" asked Tony.

"He most certainly Khan," I assured him. "It is possible, though it takes time, to teach G-nos to say G-yes. But it's rather like dancing with an octopus.

"It has to be done in two easy steps and six not-so-easy steps."

G-no Handling Technique: The Tying Them Up in G-nots Solution

STEP 1
YOU: "Can I have my cricket ball back please, Mr Miseryguts?"

STEP 2
(Wait for Mr Miseryguts to take your cricket ball from his mouth.)

STEP 3
YOU: "Oh please!"

STEP 4
YOU: "Are you saying I can't have my ball back?"

STEP 5
YOU: "What, I can't have my ball back?"

STEP 6
YOU: "You mean I *can* have my ball back?"

STEP 7
(Wait for neighbour to break down, utterly confused.)

STEP 8
YOU: "Thanks, Mr Miseryguts!"

(Neighbour gives your ball back just to get rid of you.)

WARNING!!!!!
When neighbour does throw ball back, stand well clear!

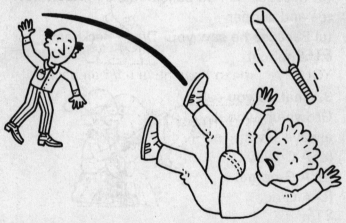

We crept out of the hide and I led Anna, Barry and Tony on towards the scariest part of the park. "It's nearly time to meet some Wildest Grown-ups," I told them. "But before we do that, we've got to do this..."

The Scarlet Pimplenose's Test on Even Wilder Grown-ups

1. How would a Wally-by Grown-up define hip hop?
(a) "It's an Easter bunny."
(b) "It's what you do if you drop a brick on your foot."
(c) "It's a kind of music."

2. Why was the Kanga-rude?
(a) Because he had baked beans for dinner.
(b) Because he had baked beans for dinner, tea and supper.
(c) Because he saw your David Beckham-style haircut.

3. What do you call a Grown-up who is always saying "no"?
(a) A G-Nitwit.
(b) A G-nome.
(c) A G-no.

ANSWERS:
1. (a) A typical Wally-by answer. Take 5 points.
(b) Another typical Wally-by answer. Take another 5 points.
(c) A Wally-by would never know this.

2. (a) Possibly.
(b) Possibly.
(c) Most likely. Take 5 points.

3. (a) G-no
(b) G-no
(c) G-yes. Take 5 points

HOW DID YOU SCORE?
10–20 points: Great! You're ready to face the Wildest Grown-ups now!

0–10 points: Hmmm... You can face the Wildest Grown-ups if you like, but I won't hold myself responsible for your safety.

How To Handle Grown-ups: Stage Four

The Wildest Grown-up

And so we approached Level Three, where the sun rarely shone and where the foliage was like Anna's friend Barry, ie very thick indeed.

"I don't like it," said Barry.

"What? The dark, you mean?" I asked.

"No, you saying I'm thick," said Barry.

On and on we trekked right into ... the darkest part of the park ... and suddenly, there in front of us, was a truly hideous sight.

It was a woman with piercing eyes and a nose as long and as bent as a banana.

"Mummy!" I yelled.

"My little Pimplenose," she said. "Is it really you?"

"No, Mummy, it's not me," I said. "It's someone completely different."

"Don't be a silly-billy," said my mummy. "I'd recognize that red pimple anywhere! Now aren't you going to introduce me to your young friends here?"

"A-a-a-a…" stammered Anna.

'Ba-ba-ba," stuttered Barry.

"T-t-t-t…" mumbled Tony.

"Aha, Baba and Terter. What nice names!" said my mummy, smiling so broadly her banana nose almost became a banana-split nose. "And what are you getting up to today?"

"Learning how to ha-ha–" began Tony, before I kicked him on the shin.

"Well, be sure to come and tell me all about it," said my mummy. "It sounds a lot of fun, learning to ha-ha. Now make sure you don't get into trouble!"

And with that – thankfully – my mummy marched off.

"Poor old Scarlet Pimplenose. I didn't realize your mum was a Wildest Grown-up," said Anna.

"It's not the sort of thing you like to discuss in public," I replied.

"What species of Wildest Grown-up is she?" asked Tony.

"She is what is known as a Spy-me Anteater," I said. "Let me fill you in on the gruesome details."

Wildest Grown-up Species No. 1: The Spy-me Anteater

SPINY ANTEATER

SPY-ME ANTEATER

"Spy-me Anteater Grown-ups are Grown-ups who are always *spying* on you," I explained. "They want to know what you're doing, even if it's none of their business. They are *so* nosy!"

Barry nodded. "Yes, we saw your mummy, so we know what you mean."

"Most Spy-me Anteater Grown-ups are family or carers," I went on, "and their characteristics have evolved over millions of years. This diagram of a Spy-me Anteater shows you just how well-developed they are for spying on you."

THE SPY-ME ANTEATER

A Grown-up sister's piercing eyes for peering through the cover of your secret diary.

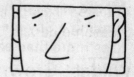

A Grown-up sister's ears for picking up your secret phone conversations.

He wants to take me to the disco...

And, of course, that nose on a mum for sniffing out anything of interest.

Oi! Have you been cleaning your bike in your bedroom again?

A gran's strong arms for hanging off the eaves of houses – there's nothing a Spy-me Anteater gran likes more than eaves-dropping.

 A dad's specially developed soft soles for creeping up on you.

Ah, going out to play without having done your homework first?

"That all looks so familiar," said Tony.

"Very familiar," added Barry.

"So, is there any way of handling these fiendish Wildest Grown-ups?" asked Anna with a sigh.

"Of course there is," I replied. "It's called..."

The Ultimate Spy-me Anteater Handling Technique

"The key to this technique lies in the previous diagram," I explained. "What you need to do is to prevent the Spy-me Anteater Grown-up from using any of their well-developed characteristics. Like this..."

A Grown-up sister's piercing eyes for peering through the cover of your secret diary – attach two springs to page one of your diary. Not one, but two in the eye for the Spy-me Anteater!

A Grown-up sister's ears for picking up your secret phone conversations – use the new Knockia 2000. When you flip it open, its telescopic cover knocks any unwanted listeners on the head.

And, of course, that nose on a mum for sniffing out anything of interest – a liberal sprinkling of pepper around your bed should do the trick!

A gran's strong arms for hanging off the eaves of houses – there's nothing a Spy-me Anteater gran likes more than eaves-dropping.

Never heard of superglue? That'll give you a break from her eaves-dropping for a day or two.

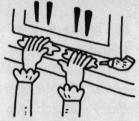

A dad's specially developed soft soles for creeping up on you – what else do you think ball-bearings are for?

"That's brilliant, Scarlet Pimplenose," said Anna. She frowned. "There aren't any disadvantages with this technique are there?"

"Just the five," I said.

Disadvantages of this Technique

1. You may forget what you've put in your diary next time you go to write in it.

2. It's only too easy to hold the Knockia 2000 too close to *your* ear.

3. Pepper is no respecter of noses.

4. Your eaves-dropping granny might well pull the guttering off, just as you are standing underneath.

5. Have you any idea just how fast a dad can go when propelled by ball-bearings? The words "flat out" just don't begin to describe it.

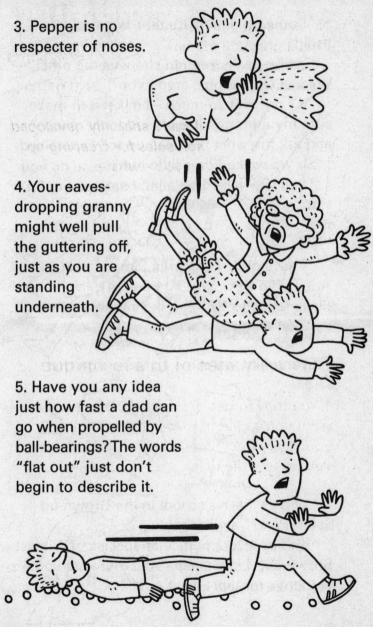

"Come on, I think it's time we moved on," I said.

"You're really keen to show us the other Wildest Grown-ups, aren't you?" said Barry.

"It's not that so much – I'm keen to make sure my mummy doesn't suddenly reappear and ask me what I've been up to," I explained.

So we walked on a little more.

Then we walked on a little moor.

Eventually, we came across a sign that said:

"Why is there a school in the Grown-up Safari Park?" asked Tony.

"It's home to a particular species of Wildest Grown-up," I explained. "And there are some of them over there right now!"

Wildest Grown-up Species Nos. 2–6: The School Caretaker and his Cleaners

"It's a School Caretaker and his Cleaners!" I shouted. "Out of the way, before we're all sucked up into that turbo-charged 1000cc vacuum cleaner or are beaten about the ankles by that giant broom! Come on, let's hide behind this tree!"

"I'm not hiding behind any more trees," said Anna angrily.

"OK," I said.

So we hid in front of the tree, instead. Luckily, the Caretaker and his Cleaners were far too busy hoovering the playground to notice us. When they eventually zoomed off out of sight, I sat Anna, Barry and Tony down and began to instruct them in the mysteries of the School Caretaker and his Cleaners.

"Now for some reason that even top scientists are trying to fathom, Caretakers and their Cleaners like schools," I said. "Already, research has been carried out to find out what School Caretakers' and Cleaners' fave buildings of the world are. These are the results..."

School Caretakers' and Cleaners' Top Buildings of The World

3. THE TRIFLE TOWER

2. THE LEANING TOWER OF PIZZA

1. MY SCHOOL!

"Unfortunately Caretakers and Cleaners don't have the same kind of enthusiasm for the people who use schools. The trouble is, when people use schools they make them grubby and dirty and that's what the School Caretaker and his Cleaners hate."

"Caretakers and Cleaners become really difficult to handle if they think their school is under attack. And, like any creature who thinks its territory is under attack, they have their own cries of alarm. Here are some typical Caretaker and Cleaner cries of alarm. Together with a suggestions of the way it's best *not* to respond."

How *Not* to Handle a School Caretaker and his Cleaners

CARETAKER'S OR CLEANER'S CRY	WHAT *NOT* TO SAY/DO
(As you walk in from the football pitch) "Don't walk across that floor with those muddy feet!"	"OK! I'll walk across the ceiling."

RESULT: This drives the Cleaner up the wall.

| (To you as you walk back from lunch holding an empty sour-cream-and-onion crisp packet) "In the bin with that!" | "OK!" You proceed to jump into the litter-bin with the crisp packet. |

RESULT: The Caretaker goes bananas. You go "Bananas!" Rotten, soggy ones that were lying in the bottom of the litter-bin and are now squelching into your trainers.

(As you amble by reading a copy of *How To Handle Grown-ups*) "Watch that bucket of water!"

"OK!" You stand there and watch the bucket of water for the next three hours.

RESULT: This drives the Cleaner crazy and the Cleaner drives her vacuum cleaner – right at your legs, which are already smelly and squelchy from having stood in a litter-bin full of rotten bananas (see above).

The School Caretaker and his Cleaners Handling Technique: The Use-a-Teacher Solution

"If there's something that annoys a School Caretaker and his Cleaners more than children," I explained, "it's teachers. They think that teachers have been put on earth just to make life difficult for them."

"That's stupid," said Barry.

"Of course it is," agreed Anna. "Teachers have been put on earth just to make life difficult for *us*."

"True," I agreed. "But just try telling that to a Caretaker or Cleaner. On the other hand, don't. It would only provoke them. The point is, if you find yourself having trouble with a Caretaker or Cleaner, simply blame a teacher!"

"Can you give us an example?" asked Tony.

So I did.

"My very best egg samples," I said.

"Your very worst joke," muttered Anna.

"Oh no it's not," I replied. "My very worst joke is the one about the budgerigar and the food blender. You see, there was this budgerigar—"

"We don't want to know!" chorused Anna, Barry and Tony. "We want to know how to use a teacher to handle a School Caretaker and his Cleaners!"

"OK!" I said.

How to Use a Teacher to Handle a School Caretaker and his Cleaners

CARETAKER'S OR CLEANER'S CRY	WHAT *NOT*TO SAY/DO
(As you walk in from the football pitch) "Don't walk across that floor with those muddy feet!"	"But Mr Hardnut* told us to go in and get changed!"

*ie your PE teacher

RESULT: Cleaner launches full-scale Mr Hardnut search.

To you as you walk back from lunch holding an empty sour-cream-and-onion crisp packet) "In the bin with that!"

"But it's part of my food tech project for Ms Crumble*!"

*ie your food tech teacher

RESULT: The Caretaker fumes, "Just you wait till I find that Ms Crumble!" And off he goes. IMPORTANT ADVICE: Don't bother to wait till the Caretaker *has* found Ms Crumble. Just get out of there!

(As you amble by reading a copy of *How To Handle Grown-ups*) "Watch that bucket of water!"

(Puzzled frown) "Are you sure that's water? Only it looks just like the bucket Mr Whizzbang* keeps his nitroglycerine in."

*ie your science teacher

RESULT: The Cleaner runs a mile.
NB: You'd be advised to do the same thing –
in the opposite direction.

aargh!

We were almost at the end of our tour
through the Grown-up Safari Park.

"What does your watch say?" I asked
Barry.

Barry stared hard
at his wrist and
frowned. "'My
very first Thomas-
the-Tank-Engine
watch'," he said.

"I meant, what's
the time?"

"Oh," said Barry. He stared hard at his
wrist again and frowned. "Nine o'clock.
Unless I've got my watch on upside-down, in
which case it's half-past three."

"Then it's almost time to get a sighting of
our very last Wildest Grown-up," I replied.
"Over there, by the school gates."

Anna, Tony and Barry let out a gasp.

Then they let it back in again.

Wildest Grown-up Species No. 7: The School Double Crossing Lady

"That's not a scary Wildest Grown-up," declared Anna. "That's a School Crossing Lady. They're very kind and help you cross the road to school."

The School Crossing Lady smiled at us.

"Yes, it is a School Crossing Lady," I said. "But you're wrong – they're the sneakiest Wildest Grown-ups known, not only to mankind, but moonkind and meankind as well."

MANKIND   MOONKIND   MEANKIND

"That's why," I went on, "it's more accurate to call them School *Double* Crossing Ladies."

"Why is that?" asked Tony.

"She may look like a nice lady, but look at the sign she's carrying."

73

"That's what School Crossing Ladies – and Men – are really about. They encourage other Grown-ups to STOP CHILDREN doing anything."

Anna, Tony and Barry looked shocked and appalled.

"I think it's time we said goodbye to the Grown-up Safari Park," I said.

"Goodbye, Grown-up Safari Park!" said Barry.

"Come on back to Tenby Gardens," I said, "and I'll show you some evidence of what the STOP CHILDREN campaign has been getting up to."

Back through Level Three, Level Two and Level One we ran, until we were back at the entrance to the Safari Park.

Anna, Barry and Tony got back on the luxury couch.

"OK, push!" shouted Anna.

I pushed. Nothing happened. Then I realized: it had been all downhill coming to the Safari Park. This could mean only one thing: it was all *uphill* going back!

Eventually, we arrived back at Tenby Gardens. When we got inside I booted up my computer. It wouldn't start, so I booted it up again.

Up on to the screen came the STOP CHILDREN home page.

DO YOU WANT TO STOP
CHILDREN RUINING THE PEACE
AND QUIET OF YOUR LIVES?
THEN JOIN US, THE

STOP CHILDREN

CAMPAIGN

- ARE YOU FED UP WITH NOISY CHILDREN
  OUT ON YOUR STREETS? WE SAY
  CONFINE CHILDREN TO THEIR HOMES
  (except between the hours of 8.15 and 8.45
  when they are going to school)
- DO YOU THINK THERE'S TOO MUCH
  CHILDREN'S TELEVISION? WE SAY NO
  MORE CARTOONS, LOTS MORE
  RICHARD AND JUDY!
- WE ALSO SAY DOUBLE NOT HALF-PRICE
  FOR CHILDREN TO ALL THEME PARKS!!!

"Seen enough?" I asked.

They had.

"Well, by way of some gentle relaxation, I've got this for you," I said, with a smile.

"NOT ANOTHER TEST!"

The Scarlet Pimplenose's Test on Wildest Grown-ups

1. Which of the following is a Wildest Grown-up?
(a) A Spiky Odoureater
(b) A Spotty Overeater
(c) A Spy-me Anteater

2. Which of the following apparently not particularly useful things can help you handle the School Caretaker and his Cleaners?
(a) A Tea Pot
(b) A Tea Chest
(c) A Tea Cher

3. Why did the School Crossing Lady cross the road and then go back again?

(a) To help a chicken
(b) Because she'd left her lollipop on the other side.
(c) Because she was a Double Crosser!

ANSWERS:
1. (a) Wrong by a couple of feet. No points
(b) Wrong by a couple of hundred kilos. No points
(c) Right. Take 5 points

2. (a) A really tea-potty answer. No points
(b) Only if it's white and you use it as a flag to surrender. No points
(c) Surprising but true. Take 5 points

3. (a) Eggs-traordinarily wrong. No points
(b) If you believe that you're not so much a lollipop as a wally-pop. No points
(c) Right. Take 5 points

WHAT YOUR SCORE MEANS:
15 points – you're a cool dude!
5–10 points – you're a cool dud.
0 points – you're just a dud.

"Now I can't let you all go without giving you some advice on Advanced Grown-up Handling Techniques," I said.

"Can't you?" asked Barry.

"Well, I could, but you wouldn't thank me for it," I replied.

"No, I don't suppose we would if you hadn't actually given it to us," reasoned Tony.

This conversation was making my head hurt.

"Actually, Scarlet Pimplenose," said Anna, "there's one question that's been puzzling me all day. It's about those special sorts of Grown-ups, aunts and uncles."

"Surely you don't need help handling your aunts and uncles?" I asked.

"Oh no, of course not!" replied Anna. "It's just … why are aunts called aunts and uncles called uncles?"

"I'm glad you asked me that," I said. "Because it's the title of the very next chapter."

How To Handle Grown-Ups: Stage Five

Why are Aunts Called Aunts and Uncles Called Uncles?

Simple, really...

Aunts *(n)* – another way of spelling *aren'ts*, because aunts – particularly elderly ones – are people who are fond of saying things like:

Aren't you like your mum?

Aren't you going to kiss me goodbye?

Uncles *(n)* – It looks an odd word, but it isn't really. Not when you realize that uncles are the most un-cool people on Planet Earth. They can even be more uncool than dads! They don't know the meaning of the word "cool". Take a look at this recent Un-cool Uncle survey.

Un-cool Uncle Survey

A sample of typical uncles were asked the following questions:

1. What do you think is a really cool sound?

1% answered "Kylie"
99% answered "chattering teeth"

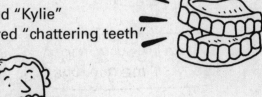

2. What do you think is cool gear?
1% answered "5th gear"
99% answered "a string vest"

3. What do you think is a really cool meal?
1% answered "Dinner for two in the chest freezer"
99% answered "frozen pizza"

How To Handle Grown-ups: Stage Six

Advanced Technique No. 1: Sneak Charming

Sneak Charming enables you to turn unreasonable Grown-ups into totally sensible people, ie people who will let you have what you want. It works like this:

Your utterly unreasonable child-minder won't let you watch *Revenge of the Killer Zombie Werewolf Vampires II*.

TIME FOR SOME SNEAK CHARM...

YOU SAY:
"Words can't describe how beautiful you look."

(This is true – words like freaky, weird, uncool don't begin to describe it)

YOUR CHILD-MINDER SAYS:
"Oh really? Now what was that film you wanted to see?"

Y-e-e-e-ah!

Your utterly unreasonable next-door neighbour is unlikely to let you get your remote uncontrolled Thunderbird 3 from his garden without a few very angry words – particularly as it's crashed through his greenhouse.

TIME FOR SOME SNEAK CHARM...
YOU SAY:
"How nice your garden looks, Mr Froggitt, much better than our dad's."

(Given that your dad's garden could win first prize in the Council Dump of the Year competition, this isn't saying a lot.)

MR FROGGITT SAYS: "What an intelligent and observant young man you are! Would you like me to get your remote uncontrolled Thunderbird 3 from my greenhouse for you?"

Y-e-e-e-ah!

Your uncool uncle needs reminding what a deserving cause you are when it comes to dishing out the dosh.

TIME FOR SOME SNEAK CHARM...

YOU SAY:
"Wow, Uncle! What a kick! Amazing isn't the word for it!"

(This is true – pathetic is more like the word for it.)

RESULT: When your uncle goes home, you get the biggest pay out ever!

Y-e-e-e-ah!

How To Handle Grown-UPS: Stage Seven

Advanced Technique No. 2: The Bribrary

A library is a place where you can find lots of very useful books. A bribrary is a place where you can find lots of very useful *bribes*. For example:

A Bribe for a Grown-up Sister's Boyfriend

The Problem: Your Grown-up sister is being taken bowling by her boyfriend Darren. You want to go with them, but they are strangely reluctant to agree to your request.

The Solution: YOU SAY to Darren: "Tell you what, if you and my sister take me bowling with you, I won't mention what happened between you and her best friend Melissa Freebody."*

The Result: Boyfriend goes very pale and agrees to take you bowling!

*Of course you've no idea what Darren got up to with Melissa Freebody, but he doesn't know that!

A Bribe for a Child-minder/Au Pair/Baby-sitter or Other Grown-up Who's Looking After You While Your Parents Are Out for the Evening:

The Problem: This annoying person expects you to go to bed before midnight!

The Solution: YOU SAY: "Tell you what, you let me stay up and I won't tell my mum and dad about the phone calls you've been making to Venezuela."*

The Result: Child-minder/Au Pair/Baby-sitter goes very pale and lets you stay up.

*Of course you don't know that the Child-minder/Au Pair/Baby-sitter has been using your mum and dad's phone to ring obscure South American countries, but apparently all Child-minder/Au Pair/Baby-sitters do it.

A Bribe for a Nosy Neighbour

The Problem: This nosy neighbour has seen you tipping buckets of mud over people's cars and then go knocking on their doors offering to clean their cars for them. He's threatened to tell your dad! Could mean big trouble.

The Solution: YOU SAY: "Tell you what, Mr Snook. You keep quiet about my car-washing scam and I'll keep quiet about the body Mrs Snook's got buried under your patio."*

The Result: Mr Snook goes pale and quickly agrees to your suggestion.

*Think this is a bit far-fetched? You wouldn't if you'd ever met Mrs Snook. She's descended from Vlad the Impaler and is capable of anything. A fact of which Mr Snook is only too well aware.

How To Handle Grown-Ups: Stage Eight

Advanced Technique No. 3: Hippo-notism

There's nothing more annoying than Grown-ups who are always saying, "When I was your age we ... were never rude to Grown-ups ... never watched TV ... always did as we were told ... never cheeked teachers ... always did our homework as soon as we got in from school ... never picked our noses in the car..."

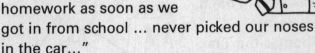

It's a load of old phoo-ey of course. The Grown-ups you know all behaved outrageously when they were young. Hippo-notism will help you find out just *how* badly...

1. Take this Hippo Book.
2. Tie a piece of string on to it.
3. Swing it in front of a Grown-up's face.

4. Say: "You are feeling sleepy ... very, very sleepy."

5. As soon as they are asleep, ask the Grown-up: "And what did you do when you were young?"

6. The Grown-up says: "Did I ever tell you about the time I put a firework under our teacher's chair?"

The Result: This Grown-up for one will never complain about *your* behaviour again!

When I had finished explaining all about Hippo-notism, Tony said, "Let's give a big hand to The Scarlet Pimplenose!"

So they did. It was the big hand off Barry's Thomas-the-Tank-Engine watch.

"We must be going," said Anna. "We've got Grown-ups to handle!"

"Well, don't go without these," I said.

And I gave them all a copy of their very own...

How To Handle Grown-ups
Personal File (Highly Confidential)

WILD GROWN-UPS I KNOW:

1.   WATER DUFFER-LOES
....
....
....

2.   YAK-ERTY-YAKS
....
....
....

3.   MOAN-KEYS
....
....
....

EVEN WILDER GROWN-UPS I KNOW:

1.   WALLY-BIES
....
....
....

2.   KANGA-RUDES

....

....

....

3.   G-NOS

....

....

....

WILDEST GROWN-UPS I KNOW:

1.   SPY-ME ANTEATERS

....

....

....

2.   SCHOOL CARETAKER
      AND HIS CLEANERS

....

....

....

3. DOUBLE CROSSING LADY/MAN

....

....

....

SNEAK CHARMS I HAVE USED:

DESCRIPTION OF SNEAK CHARM
1..
2..

NAME OF GROWN-UP USED ON
1..
2..

HOW SUCCESSFUL WAS IT (OUT OF TEN)
1..
2..

MY FAVE BRIBES FROM THE BRIBRARY:

DESCRIPTION OF BRIBE
1..
2..

NAME OF GROWN-UP IT WAS USED ON
1..
2..

HOW SUCCESSFUL WAS IT (OUT OF TEN)
1..
2..

SPECIAL AUNT AND UNCLE APPENDIX

NAME OF AUNT

1..

2..

3..

"Aren'ts" she says

1..

2..

3..

NAME OF UNCLE

1..

2..

3..

Un-cool things he says/does/wears

1..

2..

3..